Extreme Survival Stories: Kids Who Made It

Curiosity Chronicles Publishing

Published by Curiosity Chronicles Publishing, 2024.

While every precaution has been taken in the preparation of this book, the publisher assumes no responsibility for errors or omissions, or for damages resulting from the use of the information contained herein.

EXTREME SURVIVAL STORIES: KIDS WHO MADE IT

First edition. November 18, 2024.

Copyright © 2024 Curiosity Chronicles Publishing.

ISBN: 979-8230696278

Written by Curiosity Chronicles Publishing.

Extreme Survival Stories: Kids Who Made It

Real accounts of young people who survived incredible situations, with practical survival tips

Table of Contents

The Great Wilderness Adventure

(1) - Lost in the Woods: A True Story

(2) - Key Decisions: What to Do First

(3) - Consulting the Experts: Survival Professionals Weigh In

The Power of Preparation

(1) - Essential Gear Checklist for Young Adventurers

(2) - Learning Basic Survival Skills

(3) - Creating a Survival Plan with Your Family

Battling the Elements

(1) - Surviving a Sudden Storm: A Teen's Account

(2) - The Importance of Shelter: Building Basics

(3) - Expert Tips: Weather Forecasting in the Wild

Animal Encounters: A Test of Nerve

(1) - Face to Face with Wildlife: A Hair-Raising Story

(2) - Identifying Animal Tracks and Signs

(3) - Responding to Animal Encounters Safely

Finding Food and Water

(1) - An Urban Adventure: Foraging in the City

(2) - Water Sources: Identifying and Purifying

(3) - Survival Cooking Techniques for Young Chefs

The Value of Teamwork

(1) - A Group Effort: Surviving Together

(2) - The Roles of Leadership and Communication

(3) - Trust Building Activities for Adventurers

Navigating Without a Compass

(1) - Lost in the Desert: A Teen's Journey

(2) - Using Landmarks and Natural Signs

(3) - Mapping Your Route: Understanding Directions

Overcoming Fear: Mental Resilience

(1) - Staying Calm Under Pressure: Real Stories

(2) - Techniques to Build Confidence and Resilience

(3) - How Mindfulness Can Help in Survival Situations

Emergency Signals: Getting Help

(1) - A Signal for Help: The Stranded Hiker

(2) - Understanding SOS: Signaling Techniques

(3) - When and How to Call for Help Effectively

Diving into Danger: Water Survival

(1) - A Close Call in the Rapids: A True Tale

(2) - Swimming Safety Tips for Young Adventurers

(3) - Creating a Floatation Device from Nature

Handling Injuries in the Field

(1) - Unexpected Injuries: A Camper's Story

(2) - First Aid Basics Every Kid Should Know

(3) - When to Seek Professional Medical Help

The Importance of Staying Informed

(1) - Technology in the Wild: Good or Bad?

(2) - Understanding Survival Apps and Tools

(3) - Preparing for the Unexpected: Stay Updated

Hiking Safety: Know Before You Go

(1) - A Family Hike Turns Hazardous

(2) - Planning Your Hike: Safety Checklist

(3) - Trail Etiquette: Staying Safe and Respectful

Survivor Stories: Lessons Learned

(1) - Tales of Heroism from Young Survivors

(2) - Analyzing Key Decisions Made During Crises

(3) - How Survival Stories Inspire Future Generations

The Journey Ahead: Lifelong Survival Skills

(1) - Continuing Your Adventure: Resources for Learning

(2) - Building a Community of Young Adventurers

(3) - Embracing Outdoor Experiences Safely

The Great Wilderness Adventure

Lost in the Woods: A True Story

This is a gripping account of a young adventurer named Jamie, who found themselves facing an unexpected challenge in the wilderness. On what was meant to be a fun camping trip with friends, Jamie decided to explore a nearby trail alone. The lush green trees and the sound of chirping birds were inviting, but suddenly, everything felt different. The path that seemed clear began to twist and turn, leading deeper into the woods. Before long, Jamie realized they had wandered off the beaten track. Panic started to creep in. The excitement of adventure faded, and a wave of fear washed over them as the realization set in: they had lost their way.

As darkness began to fall, Jamie tapped into their instincts, remembering things they had read about survival. They took a deep breath to calm their racing heart and started thinking clearly about what to do next. Fear can cloud judgment, but Jamie recalled important survival tips that had been taught before. Finding a safe place to rest was priority number one. They selected a flat area away from potential danger, like falling branches or flooding. Gathering dry leaves and small branches, Jamie made a makeshift bed to keep off the cold ground. Staying calm and focused, they used their limited supplies wisely. Jamie reminded themselves of the importance of water and decided to listen for sounds of a stream nearby. Instead of letting fear control them, Jamie chose to rely on their instincts and the skills they had learned about navigational techniques.

Understanding mental resilience became a vital part of Jamie's survival story. They knew that staying positive was just as crucial as finding food or shelter. Reminding themselves that help would come, Jamie focused on small manageable goals. This helped shift their mindset from despair to determination. As they spent that first night in the woods, they practiced staying alert and quiet, listening for familiar sounds that might lead them back to the campsite. The experience tested their ability to navigate fear, making them stronger and more resourceful. Jamie's journey teaches us that preparation and mental strength are key elements in any adventure. Always remember to carry a map and compass, even if you think you'll just be taking a quick trip, because unexpected challenges can happen to anyone.

Key Decisions: What to Do First

When you find yourself in a challenging situation, the first step is to take a deep breath and assess what is happening around you. It's crucial to remain calm, even if your heart is racing. Panic can cloud your judgment, making it harder to see the best path forward. Look around: What does the environment look like? Are there any immediate dangers? Assessing your situation helps you gather crucial information that will inform the decisions you need to make.

Understanding your surroundings is more than just noticing what's there; it involves evaluating your resources too. What do you have with you? Food, water, tools, or even a map could be vital to your survival. Think about how you can use these resources. Remember, each situation is different, so the more you observe, the better prepared you'll be to take the next steps.

Once you've assessed your situation, you need to make some important choices. One of the first decisions is whether to stay put or move. Sometimes, the best option is to remain where you are. If you are injured, staying in one place makes it easier for rescuers to find you. Plus, moving around could lead you to more dangerous situations or deplete your resources quickly.

If you decide to stay put, you should focus on making yourself visible to potential rescuers. Use bright colors from your clothing or any gear you have to signal for help. Setting up a small fire can also serve as a signal, but only if it's safe to do so. Make sure you'll have enough materials to keep it controlled and avoid spreading a fire in a wilderness area.

If staying put doesn't feel right or you have to move, plan your route carefully. Think about the direction you want to go and avoid risky terrains, like steep cliffs or dense forests, where you could get lost or hurt. Use landmarks to navigate; mountains, rivers, or even the sun can help guide your path. Always keep awareness of your surroundings as you move, looking out for any signs of other people or areas that might offer help.

Another critical step is to communicate. If you have a phone or a whistle, use them to call for help. Sound carries in the wilderness, so if you're in a group, establish a signal that everyone understands to avoid confusion.

Throughout this process, remember that staying mentally resilient is as important as the physical actions you take. Keeping a positive mindset, focusing on your strengths, and trusting your abilities can make all the difference when facing tough situations.

In any unexpected scenario, preparation is key. Always pack a small survival kit when heading outdoors, including a whistle, a small first-aid kit, and a flashlight. These items can be invaluable when every second counts.

Consulting the Experts: Survival Professionals Weigh In

Survival experts teach us that staying safe in the wild starts with preparation. One of the most critical techniques is learning how to read the environment. This means paying attention to the weather, the terrain, and even the wildlife around you. Experts emphasize that understanding the signs of changing weather can help you avoid dangerous situations like sudden storms or dropping temperatures. For example, a shift in wind direction or darkening clouds can signal an approaching storm. Recognizing these signs can give you time to find shelter or return to safety. Carrying a small weather radio can be an invaluable tool, allowing you to stay informed if you're out for an extended period.

Another important technique is mastering the use of basic survival tools. Knowing how to create shelter, build a fire, and find water are essential skills. Experts suggest practicing these skills before embarking on an adventure. For instance, learning how to construct a debris hut can provide you with warmth and protection if you get stuck overnight. Building a fire isn't just about warmth; it also serves as a signal for help and provides comfort in unsettling situations. When learning to find water, look for streams, rivers, or even plant roots that store moisture. Remember, staying calm and using your knowledge wisely are key to survival.

Applying survival skills in real life can be exciting and empowering for young adventurers. Imagine you are hiking with friends and decide to explore a new trail. It's essential to practice what you've learned. If you accidentally wander off the path, remember the three steps: stop, think, and act. First, stopping allows you to assess your surroundings. Look for landmarks that you recognize or listen for sounds that might guide you back, like running water. Next, think about the last known point where you were with your group and consider retracing your steps.

Another helpful piece of advice is practicing the buddy system. When you're out in the wild, always travel with at least one other person. This way, you have support if something goes wrong. If a buddy gets injured, the other can help or go for help. Maybe during a camping trip, you and your friends could take turns being the designated navigator to ensure everyone stays aware of their surroundings. This not only enhances your group dynamics but reinforces the importance of teamwork in challenging situations.

In any adventure, understanding mental resilience is invaluable. Learning how to stay positive during tough moments can often make the difference between panic and calm. Experts recommend having a mental checklist of things to do if you find yourself in trouble, such as breathing exercises or focusing on what you can control. By developing these skills, you prepare not just your body but your mind for whatever adventure awaits you.

The Power of Preparation

Essential Gear Checklist for Young Adventurers

When you set out for an outdoor adventure, having the right gear can make all the difference. It's not just about being prepared; it's about being safe and having fun. Start with a durable backpack that fits well. This will hold all your gear and make it easier to carry. Pack a reusable water bottle to keep hydrated, essential for any hike or camping trip. Bring along a first aid kit tailored for kids, complete with band-aids, antiseptic wipes, and anything else you might need in a pinch. A map and compass are crucial too; they teach you navigation and can be lifesavers if you get lost. Don't forget an emergency whistle. This little tool is important because it helps you signal for help without exhausting your voice. Whether you're trudging through the woods or exploring a new trail, comfortable and sturdy shoes are necessary. Choose footwear that provides ankle support and grip, helping you avoid slips and falls. On chilly days, layering is the key; pack a light jacket or a fleece to stay warm without overheating. Add a flashlight for those moments when daylight fades. A pocket knife can also be handy; just remember, it's a tool, not a toy. Finally, you should consider your own personal safety gear. Things like a helmet for biking or a life jacket for kayaking make outdoor activities safer, allowing you to enjoy your adventure without worry.

Selecting gear that fits your age and the activities you want to do is equally important. It's essential to pick items that are specifically designed for younger adventurers. Look for backpacks and equipment that are lightweight and proportioned for your body, ensuring you can carry everything comfortably. When it comes to shoes, make sure they fit well and offer proper support. Visiting a store can help you try on different brands and styles. Always keep in mind the kind of adventure you're undertaking. If you're planning to camp, search for gear that's suited for the terrain and weather. For example, a sleeping bag rated for the temperatures you might face will ensure you stay warm at night. Know your hobbies too; if you love climbing, make sure your gear includes a harness and appropriate climbing shoes. Talk to your friends or mentors about their experiences with their gear. Their insights can guide you in making the right decisions. Remember, it's not just about having the latest equipment; it's about being equipped for safety and enjoyment too.

Understanding the risks associated with outdoor adventures is important for any young adventurer. Challenges can arise, from sudden weather changes to wildlife encounters. Mentally preparing for these situations is just as important as physical preparation. Before heading out, take some time to learn about the area you'll be visiting. Inform yourself about the wildlife in the region, including any potential dangers like snakes or bears. Familiarize yourself with basic survival skills, such as how to start a fire or find clean water. Always stick to marked trails, and if you feel uncomfortable or unsure at any moment, don't hesitate to reach out for help or turn back. This is where mental resilience comes into play; staying calm can help you think clearly and handle unexpected situations. It's okay to be nervous or scared, but remember, planning and preparation can significantly reduce those feelings. Lastly, practice having fun while staying smart and safe. Your adventures will teach you valuable lessons that will help you grow, both as an adventurer and an individual.

Learning Basic Survival Skills

Every young adventurer should learn essential survival skills to thrive in the wild. One of the most crucial skills is fire-making. Having the ability to start a fire can provide warmth, cook food, and signal for help. Exploring different methods, such as using a flint and steel or even friction through a bow drill, can be both exciting and educational.

Practicing in a controlled environment, like a backyard or park, can help build confidence without the added risk of being in the wilderness. Along with fire-making, learning basic first aid can save lives. Understanding how to treat simple injuries, like cuts and scrapes, as well as recognizing more serious conditions, empowers you to act calmly in emergencies. It's important to remember that while the nature adventure is thrilling, knowing your limits and how to respond to challenges is part of being a responsible adventurer.

To make learning these skills enjoyable, simple drills can add an element of fun to the experience. Organizing a friendly competition can motivate practice. For instance, setting up a fire-building challenge where participants have a set time to create a flame can ignite excitement. Another fun drill could involve role-playing as if responding to an emergency, where one person plays the injured party and the others practice first aid skills. These engaging activities not only develop vital skills but also foster teamwork and improve communication among friends. Incorporating storytelling while practicing can enhance the learning experience, allowing young adventurers to visualize real-life scenarios while developing their survival skills.

Understanding that mental resilience is as important as physical skills cannot be overstated. Adventures may not always go as planned, presenting unexpected challenges that require a calm mind and quick thinking. Practicing mindfulness—staying present in the moment—can help manage stress and anxiety. Encourage young adventurers to find ways to stay motivated and positive, reminding them that even experienced adventurers have faced tough situations. Practicing visualization techniques in which they imagine overcoming challenges can also prepare them mentally for real-life adventures. Always remember, being prepared is the key to safety and success in any outdoor adventure.

Creating a Survival Plan with Your Family

Involving family members in disaster preparedness and outdoor safety is vital for ensuring everyone knows what to do in case of an emergency. Each family member can have a role, regardless of their age. Start by holding a family meeting where everyone gets a chance to share their thoughts. Discuss the potential dangers that might arise in your area, such as natural disasters, and what steps you can take together. Make a list of essential supplies like food, water, and medical kits, and assign tasks to each family member. For younger siblings, assign simple jobs like gathering non-perishable food from the pantry or helping to organize a first-aid kit. This gives them a sense of involvement and responsibility, making them feel important. Regularly practicing fire drills or evacuation plans can help everyone stay calm and know what to do during a real emergency. Education about outdoor safety also involves talking about safe practices like staying on marked trails, using appropriate gear, and understanding the weather before heading out. When everyone is informed and engaged, the entire family can confidently face challenges together.

Teamwork and communication are crucial for ensuring your family is prepared for any situation. Engaging in activities that promote these skills helps everyone understand their strengths and how they contribute to the group. Outdoor adventures like camping or hiking can be great ways to build these skills. While out, set challenges that require cooperation, such as building a shelter or starting a fire without matches. Discuss the plans as a team, and make sure everyone has a voice in the decision-making process. This practice not only teaches survival skills but also instills a sense of confidence and unity among family members. To enhance communication, engage in games that require listening and following instructions, like a scavenger hunt where everyone must work together to find the items on the list. Encourage open dialogue about fears and concerns related to outdoor safety, allowing everyone to express themselves. A supportive environment fosters resilience and prepares your family for the unexpected.

One practical tip to remember is the importance of making a family emergency plan. Write down your plan, including meeting spots, contact information, and emergency numbers. Post this plan in a common area of your home. Review it regularly so that it stays fresh in everyone's minds. By being proactive, your family will not only be better prepared for disasters and outdoor adventures but will also build a stronger bond through shared experiences and open dialogue. Taking these practical steps can make a significant difference when facing challenges.

Battling the Elements

Surviving a Sudden Storm: A Teen's Account

It was a regular Saturday morning, and I planned to spend the day hiking with my friends. As we packed our backpacks with snacks, water, and a first-aid kit, the weather seemed perfect—sunshine, blue skies, and a nice cool breeze. We headed into the forest, excited and ready for an adventure. Everything was going great until dark clouds suddenly rolled in, blocking the sun and casting an eerie shadow over the trees. At first, we thought it might just be a brief shower, so we continued on our path, laughing and joking. But then, the wind picked up, and we heard a rumble in the distance that wasn't just thunder; it was the sound of a storm brewing fast. Before we knew it, raindrops started falling, followed by a fierce downpour. We realized we were in the middle of a sudden storm and needed to act quickly.

In that moment, I remembered the safety tips I'd learned in school and through my outdoor clubs. We found a sturdy grove of trees to take shelter under, making sure to stay away from the tallest ones because lightning could strike. My heart raced, but I tried to stay calm and reassure my friends. While waiting for the storm to pass, I encouraged us to think about our next steps. Conversations about safety and staying together helped ease our panic. Once the rain eased, we made the decision to head back to the trailhead instead of pushing on. We knew that while we could have pressed on in better weather, safety had to come first. Fortunately, we were equipped with a map and a compass, which helped guide us back. The storm had reminded me that preparedness is key; even if we had planned for a perfect day outdoors, nature had other ideas.

Looking back, I learned that storms don't just come from clouds—they can appear in many forms, and being ready makes a huge difference. Our experience taught me valuable lessons about resilience. We had faced a tough situation, and while it felt frightening, we worked together as a team to stay safe. Moreover, these situations can often linger in our minds, causing worry about the next adventure. But one important takeaway is that staying prepared and capable builds confidence. I realized that understanding how to read the weather signs can help prevent dangerous situations. Besides carrying essential gear, like a first-aid kit and extra clothing, we needed to have a mental checklist of what to do if things went sideways. I promised myself to study more about weather patterns and survival strategies. Having the knowledge to react quickly and calmly is just as important as having the right supplies.

Another crucial aspect is communication. We found that staying connected and expressing our fears helped keep everyone calm. It reminded me that teamwork isn't just about working together but also about supporting each other emotionally. We were all scared but sharing that fear made it easier to tackle the storm. This experience solidified my conviction that mental resilience is just as important as physical preparation. Even with the suitable gear, without a calm mind, we might have panicked and made poor decisions. The next time you plan an adventure, remember that storms can hit unexpectedly. Stay prepared, be aware of your surroundings, and keep your friends close during tough times. Think about how you would react in a sudden situation, and practice those thoughts so that when a storm comes, you can stay focused and make the right choices.

The Importance of Shelter: Building Basics

In the wild, having shelter can make all the difference between comfort and discomfort, safety and danger. When you find yourself in a survival situation, the first step is to assess your surroundings and choose a suitable location. Look for a spot that is flat, dry, and ideally not too close to water, which can flood during bad weather. Start by looking for natural features like fallen trees, rock overhangs, or thick bushes that can provide some cover. Nature can provide the skeleton for your shelter, but you'll need to add your own materials to make it effective.

Once you've chosen your spot, you can begin building. A simple lean-to can be quick and efficient. Gather a long branch and lean it against a tree or another sturdy vertical structure at an angle. Then, collect smaller sticks, leaves, and other natural materials to create a wall on one side, leaving an opening for entrance and ventilation. Make sure the roof can protect you from rain and wind. Cover the lean-to with plenty of leaves, pine needles, or moss to provide insulation and camouflage. Building this way helps you work with the environment, using existing resources that make the shelter strong without needing too much effort.

Finding the right materials in nature is key to building a secure shelter. Start by looking for large branches or logs; these can be used as the main frame or walls of your shelter. Additionally, smaller branches and reeds are excellent for filling in gaps. When it comes to insulation, look for dry leaves, grasses, or pine boughs. Piling these under and on top can keep warmth in when temperatures drop. In places with snow or extreme cold, using snow to create walls can provide significant insulation.

As you gather materials, it's crucial to also consider how they can protect you from environmental hazards. Thick bushes or fallen logs can act as barriers from wind and rain. Avoid using green wood, as it doesn't provide the same level of insulation and can leak moisture into your shelter. Natural materials not only give you physical safety but can also help you remain inconspicuous in the wild, blending in with your surroundings. This quiet presence in nature is both a survival tactic and a way to appreciate the world around you.

Always remember, preparation is the key to successful shelter building. Maintain a calm mindset and keep your eyes open for resources. The wilderness is full of materials that, when used wisely, can create a safe haven.

Expert Tips: Weather Forecasting in the Wild

Nature is full of signs that can hint at changes in the weather. For example, when the sky turns dark and the wind picks up, it may signal an approaching storm. Observing how animals behave can also provide clues; birds may fly low to the ground when a storm is near, while squirrels might gather extra food before cold weather sets in. Additionally, the smell of rain can be detected before it arrives, often described as a fresh, earthy scent. This is due to a compound released from the ground that plants produce, known as petrichor. It's important to pay attention to these signs, as they can give you precious minutes to prepare for changing conditions.

Staying informed about the weather doesn't always require fancy devices. Basic tools, like a barometer or a simple thermometer, can make a big difference. A barometer helps measure air pressure, which often drops before a storm. You can also keep an eye on the clouds; different types indicate different weather patterns. For instance, fluffy, white clouds usually mean fair weather, while dark, thick clouds can suggest rain. Utilizing a weather app on your phone can also help you stay updated. In addition to these tools, regularly checking weather forecasts and listening to radio updates while out in the wilderness will help ensure safe planning for your adventures.

During outdoor adventures, being prepared for sudden weather changes is crucial. Carrying an emergency poncho, having extra layers of clothing, and knowing how to find shelter quickly can make a big difference. When planning a hike or outdoor activity, always check the weather beforehand and make sure you have a plan in case things go awry. It's about balancing excitement for adventure with safety; preparation is your best friend in the wild. Lastly, don't forget to stay calm and think critically if unexpected weather hits, because a strong mindset is key to handling any situation that arises.

Animal Encounters: A Test of Nerve

Face to Face with Wildlife: A Hair-Raising Story

Imagine walking quietly through a dense forest, the sunlight trickling through the leaves, when suddenly, you come face to face with a bear. This is the kind of moment that adrenaline kicks in, and your body goes on high alert. You might feel like running, but that could be the worst thing to do. Instead, it's crucial to stay calm. Slowly, assess the situation. Bears, especially black bears, may not be aggressive if they sense you are not a threat. In this case, backing away very slowly while keeping your eyes on the bear is essential. Creating distance allows both you and the bear to feel safer. Always carry bear spray when hiking in bear territory, and know how to use it. Make noise as you walk to alert wildlife of your presence. If you encounter a bear, speaking calmly can also help; it can recognize human voices as non-threatening.

Witnessing wildlife in their natural habitat can be awe-inspiring, but it's important to remember that these creatures are wild and unpredictable. Keeping a respectable distance is not just smart; it's crucial for your safety and theirs. Wildlife are not accustomed to humans and can feel threatened, especially if they have young ones nearby. Learning to read animal behavior is critical. For instance, if a deer raises its head and stares at you, it's sensing you. If that deer then bolts, it's best to stay quiet and still. This not only minimizes your chances of startling the animal but also allows you to enjoy the moment. Respect for wildlife goes beyond just staying safe; it's about recognizing that you are a visitor in their home.

Understanding nature's rules can empower you as an adventurer. When hiking or exploring, carry a field guide and familiarize yourself with the wildlife in the area. Knowledge is one of the best tools for safety. Think ahead about your route and make a plan, including shouldering the responsibilities of following local guidelines about wildlife encounters. If you see an animal, maintain your distance and observe quietly, using binoculars if you want a closer look. Lastly, remember that nature can be unpredictable. Preparing for the unexpected means embracing the thrill of adventure while knowing how to keep yourself and wildlife safe. Always prioritize safety and knowledge on your outdoor journeys.

Identifying Animal Tracks and Signs

Recognizing animal tracks is like solving a mystery. Each footprint tells a story about the animal that made it. To start, pay attention to the shape of the tracks. Different animals leave unique patterns. For example, deer tracks are heart-shaped, while a coyote's are more oval. Look closely at the size as well; a small track might belong to a rabbit, while a larger one could be from a bear. The surrounding environment also offers clues. Scratches on trees can indicate where animals like bears climb, while bent grass might show where deer have been feeding. Understanding these signs helps you learn about wildlife habits, including their feeding patterns, movement paths, and even their sleeping spots. Remember, tracks can be tricky. They might fade away due to rain or wind, so act quickly when you spot them. Make a habit of observing when you're outdoors—this sharpens your skills and prepares you for your next adventure.

To practice identifying these signs, try organizing a nature hike with friends or family. Bring along a notebook or your smartphone to take pictures. Challenge each other to find tracks and signs, such as nests, chew marks on wood, or scat, which is another name for animal droppings. Discuss who you think made the tracks and what they might have been doing in that area. To make it even more exciting, create a scavenger hunt. List various animal signs to look for along the trail. As you hike, share your findings and theories. This not only enhances your observing skills but also connects you deeper with nature. Make sure you stay safe while doing this. Stick to marked trails, keep a distance from any potentially dangerous animals, and always inform an adult before heading out. Knowing the basics of safety and wildlife behavior will boost your confidence and enjoyment on these outdoor adventures.

While hunting for tracks is thrilling, always remember that some animals can pose dangers. For instance, if you spot bear tracks, it's essential to give them space. This is where mental resilience comes in; stay calm and focused. A clear head will help you decide the best course of action. Knowing when to retreat and how to communicate with your group about safety is crucial. Each adventure is an opportunity not just to learn but to grow. Keeping a respect for nature and its inhabitants makes your outdoor experiences not only educational but also safe and fulfilling. Next time you're outside, take a moment to stop, look, and listen. The stories of the wild are waiting to be discovered.

Responding to Animal Encounters Safely

When you find yourself face-to-face with wildlife, it's important to know how to react to stay safe. Each animal you might encounter has different behaviors and responses. For instance, if you see a deer, enjoy the moment but keep your distance. They are generally calm, but can get startled. Back away slowly and quietly, giving it space. If you come across a bear, the situation changes. Never run, as this may trigger a chase response. Instead, stand your ground and speak firmly. If the bear approaches, try to make yourself look as big as possible. Wave your arms and make noise, but don't make direct eye contact. If the bear attacks, playing dead can sometimes be the best option for protection. On the other hand, an encounter with a snake can be alarming. Most snakes are not aggressive unless threatened. If you spot one, back away slowly to give it room to escape.

Staying calm during wildlife encounters is crucial. When fear takes over, it can lead to poor decisions that could endanger you. Take a deep breath and assess the situation. Ask yourself the basic question: how close is the animal? If you feel threatened, or the animal doesn't leave, it might be time to calmly retreat. Make your movements deliberate—quick actions can startle both you and the animal. Turning your back to a wild animal can also be risky, as they might interpret it as an opportunity to approach you. Instead, continue to face the animal while slowly stepping back to safety. This balanced approach helps you maintain control and awareness during a potentially dangerous encounter.

Finding Food and Water

An Urban Adventure: Foraging in the City

Foraging in the city can be an exciting adventure, blending the thrill of discovery with the health benefits of fresh, wild food. However, it's essential to know which plants are safe to eat and how to avoid any dangerous missteps. Start by familiarizing yourself with common edible plants like dandelions, clover, and wild garlic. These plants are often found in parks, along sidewalks, and in vacant lots. Learning to identify these plants correctly is crucial; using a field guide or a reliable app can help you distinguish edible varieties from lookalikes that might be toxic. Always remember to check for cleanliness—some areas may be sprayed with chemicals or have been exposed to pollution, so only forage from places you trust.

Before you venture out, having the right tools can make your foraging trip safer and more enjoyable. A small knife or scissors, gloves, and a basket or bag to hold your finds can help you gather your treasures without damaging the plants or harming yourself. When you're out there, pay attention to your surroundings. Being mindful of traffic and other hazards in urban areas is a must. After you've gathered some plants, it's time to prepare them. Always wash your foraged items thoroughly. If you're uncertain about a plant, it's best to err on the side of caution: do not consume it.

Foraging can be a fantastic family adventure that combines fun and education. Organizing a foraging day with your family can make it exciting for everyone involved. Start by planning your route—choose a nearby park or green space, and map it out. Engaging everyone in the planning process can make them feel more invested in the journey. You might want to turn it into a scavenger hunt where each family member looks for specific plants, keeping score of who finds the most. This game aspect not only enhances the experience but also allows each member to learn something about the plants they're seeking.

To balance excitement with safety, make it a family rule that everyone discusses what they want to forage together before picking anything. This can prevent any accidental mistakes with harmful plants. You can also turn your adventure into a learning opportunity by researching the plants and discussing their uses before you set out. When you return home, try cooking a meal with your foraged goodies. This not only brings your adventure full circle but also fosters a sense of accomplishment among family members. Remember, the goal is not just to collect but to enjoy the experience as a family.

Always maintain a respectful attitude toward nature during your foraging expeditions. It's important to leave enough of each plant for others to enjoy and to preserve the ecosystem. A great tip for beginners is to take notes on which plants you find and where. This way, you'll have a personal foraging guide to reference for future adventures, building your confidence as you learn more about the urban wilderness.

Water Sources: Identifying and Purifying

Finding safe drinking water in the wild can be a thrilling adventure, but it's essential to know where to look in order to stay hydrated. One of the best places to start is by locating natural water sources like streams, rivers, and lakes. However, not all water is safe to drink. Before you fill your canteen, remember that water can contain harmful bacteria and parasites, so purifying it is key. If you're near flowing water, such as a stream, look for spots where the water is clear and free of debris. Avoid stagnant pools, as these are more likely to harbor pathogens.

Purifying water can be done in several ways, and it's crucial to choose one that suits your situation. Boiling is one of the most effective methods. By bringing water to a rolling boil for at least one minute, you kill most microorganisms. If you're at high elevations, boil for three minutes to be safe. Another method is using a water filter. Portable filters can remove bacteria and some viruses, but make sure to check the specifications to know what it filters out. If you don't have a filter or fire, you can use chemical purification tablets that you can add to water. These tablets take about 30 minutes to work, so plan accordingly while you're out exploring.

To ensure you have clean water to stay hydrated during your adventure, preparation is just as important as finding a source. Always carry a reliable water purification method with you. A compact water filter can be a game-changer on a long hike or camping trip. Also, learning how to set up a solar still can be a handy skill. This method uses sunlight to distill water from the ground, but it takes time and is best used in sunny conditions. Practicing these techniques before your trip will make you feel more confident when it's time to put them to use.

Moreover, it's important to stay mentally prepared for scenarios when water sources are scarce. Stay aware of your surroundings and track potential water sources while on the move. If you know you will be in an area where water is limited, consider packing extra water or a collapsible water container. Remember to ration your water wisely, especially in hot weather. Always keep hydration in mind, and don't forget that safe, clean water is one of your most important tools for outdoor survival.

Survival Cooking Techniques for Young Chefs

Survival cooking is not just about great recipes; it's about using what you have around you. Many young chefs may find themselves in outdoor situations where traditional cooking gear isn't available. However, nature provides plenty of resources to whip up a meal like a pro. One of the easiest methods is using a simple fire pit. Gather dry sticks, leaves, and stones to create a safe area to build your fire. Once your fire is roaring, you can use a sturdy stick to roast foods like marshmallows or even find wild vegetables like dandelion greens to cook over the flames.

Another fantastic method is using a makeshift rock oven. All you need are flat stones to form a sort of bowl, which can hold hot coals from your fire. Place your food wrapped in leaves—such as fish or roots—in this pit. Cover it with more stones and let the heat work its magic. Not only does this method cook food evenly, but it also helps you appreciate the flavors of the earth around you. Remember, always check that what you're cooking is safe to eat, and never put anything in your mouth you can't identify.

Cooking outdoors can be a thrilling adventure, especially when you collaborate with your friends. One fun recipe to try is the "Campfire Nachos." Pack some tortilla chips in your backpack, and when you find a great spot to set up camp, layer them in a cast-iron pan or even a flat piece of aluminum foil. Add some chopped veggies, beans, and cheese if you have it, then wrap it in foil and set it over the fire for about ten minutes. The wait gets everyone excited and brings the group together as you take turns checking on your delicious creation.

Another creative dish is "Nature's Pizza." For this, gather flatbread or even large leaves from edible plants. Spread tomato sauce or any spread you have on top and sprinkle with foraged herbs or even small pieces of meat if it's safe. You can create individual pizzas, which makes it even more fun. Everyone can customize their own with the ingredients available. As you cook, talk about where the ingredients came from and how to safely gather them. Think of cooking as a way to share stories while working together, turning hunger into a delightful experience that strengthens friendships.

Remember, the joy of cooking in the wild lies not just in the food but also in the moments you share while preparing it. Stay safe, be aware of your surroundings, and always prioritize teamwork in every dish you create.

The Value of Teamwork

A Group Effort: Surviving Together

During one summer, a group of friends decided to go camping in the mountains. They were excited about spending time in nature, roasting marshmallows, and telling stories around the campfire. However, the trip took an unexpected turn when a sudden storm hit. Dark clouds rolled in, and rain began to pour down, soaking everything in moments. The friends quickly realized the importance of staying together and using their skills to navigate the dangerous situation.

As the winds howled and trees swayed, they remembered their survival training from school. One friend suggested they build a makeshift shelter to stay dry. They gathered branches and large leaves, working as a team to create a covering. Each person played a role; some held the branches, while others tied them together with cord they had packed. Thanks to their teamwork, the shelter stood strong against the storm. This experience taught them that their combined efforts were far more powerful than trying to figure things out alone.

Collaboration becomes crucial during survival situations. Each member of a group may have different skills and strengths, which can be incredibly useful. For example, one friend was excellent at starting fires, while another had knowledge of edible plants. By working together, they could gather food and build a fire to stay warm and nourished. This teamwork not only increased their chances of survival, but it also helped to boost everyone's morale. The friends shared laughter and stories even in the face of danger, creating a strong bond that helped calm their nerves.

When individuals share responsibilities, it reduces the stress that can come from trying to tackle everything alone. Each person can focus on a particular task, allowing for better organization and efficiency. One could work on gathering water, while another could check for dangers around the campsite. This way, they kept one another safe and maintained a level of alertness that is essential in risky situations. Their mental resilience was built by trusting each other and understanding that they were stronger as a unit.

Planning ahead for emergencies is crucial in any adventure. Before heading out, it's wise to designate roles for each person, practice your skills together, and discuss what to do in case of various emergencies. This type of preparation can make a significant difference when faced with unexpected hardships, allowing a group to respond calmly and effectively.

The Roles of Leadership and Communication

Every adventure teaches us about teamwork and the unique strengths each person brings to the group. When you're out in the wild, whether you're hiking, camping, or rock climbing, everyone plays a vital role. Imagine a team setting out on a hiking expedition. Each member has different skills that can help the group succeed. One person might be great at navigation, using a compass and map to keep everyone on the right path. Another might have excellent cooking skills, preparing meals that keep energy up in the group. There could be a member who excels at first aid, quickly stepping in if someone gets a scrape or bruise. These diverse talents create a supportive environment where individuals feel valued and motivated to contribute. When each person knows their role and performs it well, the group can overcome challenges more effectively.

Effective communication can be the difference between a thrilling adventure and a dangerous situation. When you're out in nature, clear communication helps everyone understand what needs to be done, especially when problems arise. Imagine you're hiking and someone slips, spraining their ankle. In that moment, it's not just about the injury, but also about making sure everyone remains calm. Using clear, concise language is key. Instead of shouting Help! you might say, We need to stop and assess the injury. This shows leadership and helps others understand the immediate priority. You can also use hand signals when sound doesn't carry as well, such as during windy days. Make sure to practice these techniques during the planning stages of your adventure. For instance, gather your team before leaving and discuss how you'll signal in case of emergencies. This preparation builds confidence and ensures everyone knows what to do when faced with unexpected situations.

Remember, staying alert and thinking ahead contribute to safety and success. Always check in with your team members during your adventure to keep everyone informed of your plans and any changes that occur. Communication isn't just about speaking; it's also about listening and observing. Pay attention to the vibes of your teammates. If someone looks uneasy or is struggling, check in with them. Building a supportive atmosphere where everyone communicates openly ensures that your adventure remains fun, exciting, and safe. Always prioritize preparation and knowledge-sharing to tackle any challenges that come your way.

Trust Building Activities for Adventurers

Engaging games and activities can create a strong bond among teammates, especially in adventure settings. One popular trust-building game is the Blindfold Challenge, where one person is blindfolded and must rely on their teammates' verbal guidance to navigate through an obstacle course. This activity emphasizes communication and the importance of listening. Additionally, The Trust Fall is another classic where individuals lean back off a ledge, trusting that their group will catch them. These activities are essential not only for fun but also for building trust and understanding each other's strengths and weaknesses. It's crucial to ensure that everyone feels safe and comfortable during these activities, as the goal is to build a supportive environment that encourages participants to take calculated risks.

Improving cooperation and morale during tough situations requires specific strategies. When adventures become challenging, clear communication becomes paramount. Establishing a signal for when someone needs help can foster a team-oriented atmosphere. This could be as simple as raising a hand or calling out a specific phrase. Another effective approach is to hold regular team check-ins, where each member shares how they're feeling about the challenge. This creates a safe space for concerns to be voiced and strengthens emotional connections among the group. Maintaining a positive attitude is especially important; encouraging words can uplift team spirit even in the most difficult moments. Practicing mindfulness techniques as a group, like deep breathing or visualizing success, can also enhance mental resilience and group unity in stressful situations.

Preparation and prevention are vital elements in adventure scenarios, and understanding the environment can save lives. Always discuss potential dangers before embarking on an adventure. This could involve researching wildlife, terrain, and weather conditions. Additionally, role-playing emergency scenarios can help everyone understand what to do in real-life crises. If the group is prepared, they will feel more confident and secure. Remember, it's not just about physical preparation; mental readiness is equally important. Developing a problem-solving mindset and focusing on the collective goal enhances teamwork and trust. Sharing these insights with others not only enriches your experience but also strengthens the bonds created through shared challenges. Always approach every adventure with a balance of excitement and caution.

Navigating Without a Compass

Lost in the Desert: A Teen's Journey

In the heart of a vast desert, far from the comforts of home, a teenager finds themselves alone, surrounded only by the rolling dunes and a fierce sun beating down from above. Navigating through this harsh landscape without a map or a GPS device becomes a true test of survival skills. With nothing but intuition and knowledge, the teen recalls tips learned from outdoor survival classes. Each step must be calculated, as the risk of disorientation is high. The vast stretches of sand and sparse vegetation can look deceivingly similar, making it hard to gauge direction. Perspective is crucial when the horizon stretches infinitely. The teen remembers that shadows can serve as a guide, always pointing to the west when the sun is high. Adapting to the environment becomes a daily mission as they begin to notice how features of the desert can help them find their way.

Using natural landmarks like distinctive rock formations and clusters of cacti, the teen creatively reorients themselves. By keeping track of these reference points, the landscape transforms from an unwelcoming blur into a navigable map. In moments of uncertainty, they take stock of their surroundings, allowing the natural features to provide clues. When encountering a dry riverbed, the teenager uses it as a guide toward the valley, knowing that water sources may lead to civilization. Analyzing the wind direction, they learn to observe how sand shifts and the patterns formed by the breeze carry information about their surroundings. Small victories like identifying a distant mountain range or following the sun's movement inspire confidence. Each successful decision not only demonstrates survival instinct but emphasizes the importance of connection to nature.

While the mind races with both excitement and fear, mental resilience emerges as one of the most critical tools. The teenager learns to manage panic by focusing on breath and breaking down decisions into manageable steps. This approach helps maintain clarity in difficult times. Staying hydrated becomes a priority, and finding shade wherever possible aids in conserving energy. Tapping into creativity, the teen starts to develop a routine, setting small goals for each day and recording thoughts and observations in a journal. This process not only keeps the spirits high but also brings a sense of control over the situation. For anyone exploring the wilderness, understanding how to stay calm and plan effectively amidst challenges is essential. By fostering a thoughtful mindset, anyone can navigate unexpected adventures with greater assurance.

Using Landmarks and Natural Signs

Using natural features like mountains, rivers, and trees can be an exciting way to navigate the outdoors. Mountains are often the most visible landmarks, standing tall against the skyline. When you're in a new area, first look around and identify the nearest mountains; their shapes and positions can help you determine where you are. Most mountains have unique profiles, and learning to recognize them can make a big difference. For example, if you see a mountain that looks like a sharp pyramid, it may help you gauge direction based on your knowledge of the landscape.

Rivers are another great navigation tool. They usually flow in a consistent direction, and knowing which way that is can guide you towards safety or familiar places. Many rivers lead to larger bodies of water, so if you follow them, you may find your way to civilization or a safe area. Pay attention to any notable bends or forks in the river; these can be referenced in maps or your mental notes as you journey onward.

Trees can also serve as navigational aids. Certain types of trees can indicate specific conditions, such as proximity to water. For instance, where there's a lot of water, you often find willows or alders. Be aware of the height and density of tree canopies; this can help you determine whether you're in a forested area or if you might be heading towards a clearing. Learning to recognize these patterns not only enhances your navigation skills but also helps you appreciate the beauty of nature as you explore.

Practicing natural navigation can be a fun way to develop survival skills while enjoying the outdoors. One interesting exercise is to create a map of your local area using only natural landmarks. Grab a notebook and head to a park or natural area. Look for a tall tree, a uniquely shaped rock, or a winding creek, and mark their locations on your paper. Then, try to find your way back to these points without using any technology. This will help you get accustomed to recognizing important features and understanding their relationships in the landscape.

Another engaging activity is to observe the sun's position at different times of the day. Take note of where the sun rises and sets; this natural cycle can help you identify directions. During the morning, the sun will rise in the east and set in the west. Using this information, try to navigate around your neighborhood or local park, using the sun as your guiding light.

Finally, consider organizing a scavenger hunt with friends. Create a list of natural items to find, like specific tree types, animal tracks, or particular plants. This fun game encourages you to explore your surroundings while sharpening your observation skills. By blending play with learning, you'll enhance your navigation abilities in a way that's dynamic and enjoyable.

Mapping Your Route: Understanding Directions

Maps are like a treasure map for adventures, showing paths, landmarks, and the lay of the land. Understanding how to read a map properly is crucial, especially when you're out hiking in nature. A topographical map, for instance, shows elevation changes using contour lines. These lines can tell you if the path ahead is going to be a steep climb or a gentle slope. Knowing this information helps in planning your hike to avoid exhausting climbs and allows you to stay safe while you enjoy the adventure.

Another important feature on maps is symbols representing landmarks like rivers, mountains, and trails. Being familiar with what these symbols mean gives a clearer picture of where you are and where you need to go. When you're out in the wilderness, there are no street signs or guides, so understanding these details can make a huge difference. Picture having a cool hiking experience by feeling confident about your surroundings. It's not just about adventure; it's about being smart and prepared too.

Creating your own map might sound challenging, but it can be thrilling and rewarding. Start by choosing a location you want to explore and take a good look at existing maps of that area. Pay attention to the main paths and natural elements like lakes or hills. After you've studied the maps, it's time to head out and mark key features as you explore. Bring a notebook and a pencil to jot down what you see along the way. You might sketch out a trail you find especially beautiful, or note a perfect spot for a picnic.

When you create your own map, think about what you need for a safe adventure. Mark your starting point, important landmarks, and routes you feel comfortable with. Consider areas where you might want to avoid, like steep hills if you're not ready for them. Putting this all together not only gets you familiar with your hiking environment but also builds your confidence. Remember, a well-planned map is a safety tool as much as it is a fun guide to your journey. Always remember that being prepared can turn a simple hike into an unforgettable adventure.

When embarking on your outdoor adventure, an essential tip is to regularly check the map during your hike. This practice helps ensure you stay on track and reminds you to be aware of your surroundings. Knowing where you are can make all the difference in emergency situations, giving you the knowledge to get back to safety when needed.

Overcoming Fear: Mental Resilience

Staying Calm Under Pressure: Real Stories

In the heart of the wilderness, kids often face unexpected challenges that test their courage. One inspiring story comes from a group of students on a field trip who found themselves lost during a hiking excursion. As the sun began to set, panic started to creep in, but one student remembered their lessons on survival. Instead of succumbing to fear, they encouraged their friends to stay calm and follow the steps they had practiced. They used their surroundings to help navigate back, identifying landmarks and following the sound of a nearby stream. By keeping a level head, they not only made it back safely but also learned a valuable lesson in teamwork and resilience.

In another remarkable tale, a young girl named Mia encountered a bear while camping with her family. Instinctively, she remembered her safety training and did not run or scream. Instead, she stood tall, made herself look bigger, and slowly backed away. Her calm demeanor helped her family to follow suit, preventing a potentially dangerous situation from escalating. This incident showed that a positive mindset can turn a fearful moment into a lesson in respect for nature and personal safety.

To maintain calm during such critical moments, it's crucial to focus on the positive aspects of the situation. Practicing mindfulness can be incredibly helpful. This encourages a mindset where kids can approach problems with clarity instead of fear. Specialists in psychology emphasize that during stressful events, taking deep breaths, counting to ten, and focusing on what can be controlled makes a big difference. This not only helps in coping with immediate dangers but also fosters long-term mental resilience, preparing young adventurers for future challenges they may encounter outdoors.

Techniques to Build Confidence and Resilience

Building mental toughness is like training your body for a challenging hike. Before you head out on your adventure, you can try some simple practices to prepare your mind. Start by visualizing the adventure. Close your eyes and imagine yourself successfully navigating through the trails, facing whatever challenges come your way with confidence. This mental rehearsal helps your brain get used to the idea of overcoming obstacles. You might also want to practice mindfulness. Take a few moments to focus on your breathing, letting go of worries. This helps clear your mind and prepares you for unexpected situations. Consider setting small goals each day leading up to the adventure. These could be as simple as going for a 15-minute walk or trying a new outdoor activity. Achieving these small goals boosts your confidence and makes the bigger challenge feel more manageable. Remember, each step you take towards your goal builds both confidence and mental resilience, making you better prepared for the real adventure.

Once you're outdoors, engaging in certain activities can further enhance your self-assuredness. Try teaming up with friends or family for group challenges. Working together to complete tasks, like setting up a tent or cooking over a campfire, fosters teamwork and builds confidence by sharing skills and experiences. If you're out in nature, challenge yourself to keep a positive mindset. When faced with a tricky trail or unexpected rain, instead of focusing on the negative, remind yourself of the tools and skills you have to adapt. Keeping a journal during your adventures can also be a helpful activity. Write about your experiences, fears, and achievements. Over time, you'll notice patterns of growth in your resilience. Lastly, learn from every experience, good or bad. After an adventure, take time to reflect. What went well? What could you improve next time? This reflection helps you learn and grow, ensuring that you'll be more prepared for your next outdoor challenge. Remember, each time you step out of your comfort zone and face the wilderness, you're building a stronger, more confident version of yourself.

Always prioritize safety while exploring. Before any activity, check your gear and environment to ensure everything is ready. Knowing how to stay safe not only reduces risks but also empowers you to tackle challenges with confidence. Prepare, stay alert, and trust in your abilities!

How Mindfulness Can Help in Survival Situations

Mindfulness is more than just a trendy word; it's a powerful tool that can keep you calm and focused during stressful events. When you find yourself in a scary situation, like getting lost in the woods or facing an unexpected challenge, your mind can quickly become overwhelmed. Mindfulness teaches you to pay attention to the present moment without judgment. This practice helps you to tune in to what's happening around you. Instead of panicking, you can use mindfulness to clear your head and think clearly. By focusing on your breathing, you can calm racing thoughts and make better decisions. This mental clarity is essential for evaluating your options and staying safe.

To incorporate mindfulness into your outdoor activities, start with simple exercises. One effective exercise is the 5-4-3-2-1 technique. As you wander outside, take a moment to observe your surroundings using your senses. Identify five things you can see, four things you can touch, three things you can hear, two things you can smell, and one thing you can taste. This practice roots you firmly in the present, drawing your attention away from fears and anxieties. You can also practice deep breathing. Inhale deeply through your nose, holding it for a few seconds, and then exhale slowly through your mouth. Doing this a few times can help your body relax, and your mind get ready for what comes next. Before heading out on an adventure, take a few moments to visualize potential challenges and mentally prepare yourself for them. This mental rehearsal can bolster your resilience, making it easier to stay calm when faced with difficult circumstances.

Experiencing a survival situation can be terrifying, but the key is to remember that you have tools to handle it. By practicing mindfulness regularly, you can build a mental space that allows you to cope with stress and make rational decisions even when situations feel dire. Remember, preparation is critical, and so is knowing how to ground yourself in the moment. The next time you venture outdoors, take these practices with you. They can make a significant difference when facing unexpected challenges, allowing you to stay composed and responsive rather than reactive.

Emergency Signals: Getting Help

A Signal for Help: The Stranded Hiker

A young hiker named Alex ventured into the mountains, excited to explore the beauty of nature. Unfortunately, while navigating a rocky path, Alex lost footing and fell, injuring a leg and making it difficult to hike back to safety. As the sun began to set, a feeling of panic started to creep in. Alone and unable to walk far, Alex realized that the only way to get help was to signal to anyone who might be nearby. With limited daylight, it was crucial to act fast. Alex recalled a survival lesson about using bright colors to attract attention. Looking around, Alex spotted a bright red backpack and decided to open it up, pulling out a vibrant orange rain poncho to create a larger signal. Spreading it out over a rock, Alex hoped that someone would see the flash of orange against the earthy tones of the wilderness.

There are various effective techniques for signaling for help in situations like Alex's. Sound is a powerful tool, so if you find yourself stranded, using a whistle can greatly increase your chance of being heard. Whistles can carry much farther than a shout, and they do not tire your voice. Similarly, creating visual signals can also help. If you have a mirror, using sunlight to create a signal can attract attention from miles away. If it's nighttime, consider having a flashlight to create flashes of light. Another technique is to arrange rocks or branches in a noticeable way to spell out SOS, or to build a small fire if safe to do so—its smoke can be seen from the air. Remember, being calm and thinking clearly when signaling is just as critical as the action itself.

Preparing in advance can be the difference between a close call and a disaster. Packing essential survival tools such as a compass, a whistle, and a small first aid kit can be lifesaving. Always share your hiking plans with someone who will not be with you, so they know where to look for you if something goes wrong. It's also important to stay mentally tough during such moments. Keeping a positive attitude and practicing patience can often be the key to making wise decisions under pressure. If you ever find yourself in a similar situation as Alex, remember that staying calm and thinking proactively about how to signal can make a world of difference.

Understanding SOS: Signaling Techniques

Creating emergency signals that stand out can be a matter of life or death. Simple methods like using bright colors, reflective materials, or making loud noises can help attract attention when you need help. For instance, if you're in the woods and find yourself lost, you can gather branches and leaves to form large letters on the ground, spelling out SOS. The letters should be as big as possible so they can be seen from the air. Additionally, if you have a whistle, using it in repeating bursts can signal your location to nearby hikers or rescuers. Incorporating items like mirrors or shiny objects can also reflect sunlight, creating sparkles that can catch the eye of someone far away.

The acronym SOS is internationally recognized as a distress signal. Although many think it stands for Save Our Souls, it actually doesn't have a specific meaning; it was chosen for its simplicity and ease of recognition. To create effective signals, it's essential to remember the three dots, three dashes, and three dots pattern of Morse code. This can be communicated visually or audibly. If you have a flashlight or a phone, turning it on and off in the same pattern can be effective at night. For daytime signaling, consider creating large shapes in the dirt using rocks or logs, again in the form of SOS. This increases the chance that someone will notice you, making the combination of creativity and resourcefulness crucial during emergencies.

Staying calm and thinking clearly in dangerous situations contributes greatly to your survival. Preparation is key; knowing these signaling techniques ahead of time can save crucial moments when you might feel overwhelmed. Practice these skills in different environments and share them with your friends so that everyone understands the importance of signaling for help. Mental resilience is an equally vital part of survival, allowing you to remain alert and focused, even when the situation feels dire. If you ever find yourself in a tough spot, remember to apply what you've learned about signaling and stay hopeful, as help may be closer than you think.

When and How to Call for Help Effectively

Knowing how to call for help can make a huge difference in dangerous situations. Start by ensuring your phone is charged and easily accessible. If you find yourself in a tricky spot, don't panic. Take a deep breath and stay calm. If you're using a mobile phone, dial the emergency number relevant to your area. In many places, this is 911 or 112. Provide the dispatcher with clear and accurate information. Tell them your location and what kind of help you need. Speak slowly and clearly, avoiding slang or jargon that they might not understand. If you're outdoors and there's no cell service, try to move to a higher elevation where you can get a signal, but do this safely. If you can't signal for help with your phone, consider using other methods, like whistles, mirrors, or brightly colored clothing, to catch attention. These tools can be vital in alerting others to your presence.

There are situations where seeking help should always be your first priority. If you or someone else is injured badly, like suffering from severe bleeding or unconsciousness, it is critical to get help immediately. Bad weather conditions, such as storms or extreme temperatures, can quickly turn a fun adventure into a dangerous scenario. If you feel lost or disoriented, don't hesitate to ask for help. It's better to ask for assistance when you're unsure than to venture blindly into the wilderness. Trust your instincts; if a situation feels wrong or unsafe, it probably is.

Emergencies can be unpredictable, and prioritizing getting help can save not just your life but also the lives of others.

Preparation is key to staying safe outdoors. Always tell someone where you're going and when you plan to return. Pack essential gear, including a map, a compass, and a first aid kit. Building mental resilience is just as important as having the right tools. In stressful situations, remaining calm and thinking clearly can help you make better decisions. When you think about how to communicate in emergencies, remember that clarity is critical. The clearer your message is, the better others can assist you. Try to visualize potential scenarios before they happen; that way, you will be better prepared to act when needed. Remember, staying aware of your surroundings and trusting your instincts can often be your best defense.

Diving into Danger: Water Survival

A Close Call in the Rapids: A True Tale

A thrilling adventure awaits when a teenager, filled with excitement, sets out to navigate the wild, rushing waters of a local river. The sun glints off the surface, and the sound of splashing water fills the air as they hop into their canoe. With the current roaring and the slippery rocks lurking beneath, every stroke of the paddle becomes a dance between thrill and caution. As the teen maneuvers through the twisting turns and sudden drops, the adrenaline rush is palpable. It's all fun and excitement until the water becomes violent, crashing against the sides of the canoe, making it sway ominously. The heart races, and in that moment, the realization hits: this isn't just an adventure; it's a test of skill and courage against nature's fierce elements.

Just when things seem to take a dangerous turn, quick thinking becomes the lifeline in this high-stakes moment. Remembering the safety tips learned before their outing, the teen makes a split-second decision to shift weight and steer towards calm waters. Preparation didn't just mean having a paddle; it encompassed knowing how to respond when faced with the unexpected. The importance of wearing a life jacket, checking equipment beforehand, and reviewing water safety couldn't be overstated. Each move becomes more than instinct; it reflects the preparation that went into planning the trip, highlighting the significance of being mentally ready for what lies ahead. Expert insight reinforces this idea, showing that mental resilience, combined with practical knowledge, plays a vital role in overcoming challenges in the wild.

The incident serves as a reminder that safety is paramount in every outdoor adventure. The teen's experience isn't just about the thrill of the rapids; it's about understanding the balance between excitement and responsibility. Engaging with nature isn't just a fun activity; it requires respect for the environment and awareness of potential dangers. This tale, while dramatic, emphasizes preparing in advance and being smart about choices on the water. Before an adventure begins, the lesson rings clear: always plan ahead, know your surroundings, and trust your instincts. These fundamental principles can make the difference between a scary moment and a safe, memorable adventure.

Swimming Safety Tips for Young Adventurers

Staying safe while swimming is super important, whether you're splashing around in a natural lake, a river, or a swimming pool. First, always swim with a buddy. It's not just more fun to be with friends, but having someone there can make a big difference if something goes wrong. Make sure you're swimming in designated areas that are monitored by lifeguards. They are trained to look out for swimmers and can help in emergencies. If you're in open water, be aware of your surroundings, including currents and waves. Knowing how to spot these can keep you from getting caught off guard. It's crucial to read the water conditions before you jump in. Signs may warn of strong currents, so pay attention and heed those warnings. If you feel tired, dizzy, or uncomfortable for any reason, don't hesitate to get out of the water. Listening to your body is key in keeping safe.

Practicing swimming techniques can turn safety measures into fun challenges. For example, playing games that focus on treading water not only keeps your skills sharp but also builds stamina. Try practicing floating on your back—it's a relaxing way to stay afloat and helps with overall water confidence. Shadowing more experienced swimmers can also provide insights into proper techniques. You might even create a mini obstacle course in a pool with friends, using floatation devices. This can teach quick reactions if you were ever in trouble. Each session, set small goals like practicing distance swimming or diving under water, which can help everyone improve. Remember, it's not just about having fun; it's also about building the mental resilience to face challenges in the water boldly.

When you're prepared for what lies beneath the surface, you can tackle the excitement of swimming head-on without fear. Ensure you have the right equipment like life jackets and goggles that fit well. Knowing how to use flotation devices can be a lifesaver if you tire out or find yourself in shallow waters. Teaching yourself specific signals to communicate with your buddy can also be a lifesaver. If one of you feels uncomfortable, a simple wave or sign can alert the other. Always keep an eye on the weather, too. Sunny days can quickly turn into storms, which change water conditions. Before jumping into any adventure, remember to look around, stay aware, and make decisions that keep safety as your top priority, all while enjoying the thrill of your aquatic journey.

Creating a Floatation Device from Nature

In situations where you find yourself near water and need a temporary flotation aid, natural materials can often come to your rescue. For instance, look for large, hollow logs or pieces of bamboo. These can be tied together using strong vines or sturdy grass to create a makeshift raft. Even a cluster of tightly packed leaves can add extra buoyancy if secured properly. If you spot a few large plastic bottles, they can also be great flotation devices; just make sure they are sealed to hold air. Always inspect your surroundings carefully, as using the right materials is crucial not just for effectiveness, but for safety as well. Knowing how to tie knots, like the bowline or clove hitch, will help keep your makeshift flotation device secure. Remember, the goal is not just to stay afloat but to do so in a safe manner until help can arrive.

Natural items can often serve as a lifeline in critical situations. For example, if you find yourself in turbulent waters, understanding how to use a fallen tree trunk can provide both stability and flotation. Nature gifts us with materials that, if used wisely, can help save lives. Pine branches, when bundled together and secured, can serve as a flotation aid due to their buoyant nature. In a survival scenario, it's essential to remain calm and think critically. Your surroundings may hold the keys to your survival. Reflect on the skills you've practiced; creativity and quick thinking can transform ordinary items into life-saving tools. Understanding your environment makes a significant difference in a crisis. Mental resilience can influence your ability to adapt and survive. Trust in what nature provides, and remember: it's not just about finding help, but using what you have at hand effectively.

When exploring the ways natural materials can assist during emergencies, it's also important to recognize the dangers involved. Water can be unpredictable, and conditions can change rapidly. If you're ever in a situation where you need to use a flotation device made from what you can find, think about the currents and the weather. Choose materials that will not only keep you afloat but also won't break down or succumb to water damage too quickly. Practicing these skills should be conducted in safe, controlled environments first, so when the time arises when you truly need them, you'll know just what to do. Always have a plan and strive to make the right decisions under pressure. Nature is on our side, but our own preparation is the true ally in survival scenarios.

Handling Injuries in the Field

Unexpected Injuries: A Camper's Story

Emma was excited for her first camping trip with friends in the mountains. The air was crisp, and the trees stood tall like green giants. Laughter filled the campsite as they set up their tents and shared stories around the fire. But during a hike the next day, everything changed. Emma climbed over a fallen log when she slipped, landing awkwardly on her ankle. The sharp pain that shot through her body made her gasp. It felt like lightning jolting through her leg, and she instantly knew something was wrong. Her friends rushed to her side, their faces painted with worry. She tried to stand, but the pain was unbearable. This wasn't just a scrape; it was an unexpected injury that turned their fun adventure into a test of quick thinking and teamwork.

While Emma lay on the ground, her friends quickly assessed the situation. They remembered what they had learned in their outdoor safety training. One friend, Jake, kept calm and checked for any visible injuries. Another friend, Sarah, retrieved the first aid kit from their backpacks, always prepared for moments like this. They carefully propped Emma's leg up on a pile of soft leaves. They knew elevation could help reduce swelling. Sarah gently wrapped a bandage around Emma's ankle, applying just enough pressure without causing more pain. Jake took charge and sent a friend back to the campsite to fetch help while another stayed close to Emma, keeping her spirits up. This experience showed them that, with the right knowledge and quick actions, they could manage an emergency. Emma felt grateful for her friends' swift response, knowing she wouldn't have to face the injury alone. In such situations, having a well-stocked first aid kit and understanding how to use it can make all the difference.

Thinking ahead and preparing for the unexpected is key when adventuring outdoors. Whether you're hiking, camping, or engaging in any physical activity, always prioritize safety. Learn basic first aid skills and ensure your group knows how to react in case of emergencies. Have a plan that includes easy access to your first aid supplies, and remember to respect the terrain you're exploring. Awareness and preparation can be your best allies—just like Emma found out on her camping trip.

First Aid Basics Every Kid Should Know

Every young adventurer should be equipped with some essential first aid skills. Knowing how to react in emergencies can turn a fearful situation into a manageable one. One of the first things to learn is how to assess the scene. This means looking around to make sure it's safe before helping anyone. Once you know it's safe, approach the injured person calmly. It's important to check their responsiveness by gently tapping their shoulder and asking if they're okay. If they aren't responding, it's crucial to call for help immediately. Don't be afraid to shout for an adult or call 911 if you have access to a phone.

Next, it's good to know how to handle basic wounds, like cuts and scrapes. Clean the wound with clean water and if there's bleeding, apply gentle pressure with a clean cloth. Keeping the area clean helps prevent infection. For more serious injuries, such as a sprain, learning how to use the R.I.C.E method—Rest, Ice, Compression, and Elevation—can be very useful. It helps reduce swelling and promotes healing. Also, understand that allergic reactions can happen, and knowing how to use an EpiPen can save someone's life. It's a little less common, but really important, especially in outdoorsy environments where you might encounter various allergens.

Imagine you're out hiking with friends when one of them trips and falls, scraping their knee badly. Here's where you can put your first aid knowledge into action. First, approach your friend calmly so they feel safe. Then, assess the injury. Is it a small scrape, or does it look worse? If it's manageable, grab your first aid kit, and clean the wound with water. If the bleeding is significant or there's dirt in the wound, you may need to use antiseptic wipes and cover it with a sterile bandage. Encourage your friend to take a break, hydrate, and make sure they're okay to continue the hike. Spending time practicing these scenarios, even through role-playing with friends or family, can help reinforce what you've learned.

For a more dramatic approach, picture this: you're having a campfire night when suddenly, someone starts choking on a marshmallow. It's more common than you think! Remember the Heimlich maneuver. Stand behind the person, wrap your arms around their waist, and give quick, upward thrusts until they can breathe again. Practicing these techniques in safe environments makes you more confident and prepared when real situations occur. The key is to stay calm. Panic can cloud judgment, so take a deep breath and remind yourself to act with care and precision. Staying mentally strong is just as important as knowing the techniques, and it can help you become a reliable first responder among your friends.

Always keep a first aid kit handy, and know how to use what's inside. Practice makes perfect, so run through these scenarios with your friends. Remember, having the knowledge and practicing often can make a big difference in a tough situation. You never know when you might need to help someone, so being ready is the best course of action.

When to Seek Professional Medical Help

Sometimes, during an adventure or even just a day at home, you may notice signs that something isn't right with your body or someone else's. These signs, often called red flags, are important to pay attention to. If someone has difficulty breathing, feels intense chest pain, or suddenly can't move part of their body, these are critical signals that immediate help is needed. Other red flags can include severe headaches, persistent vomiting, or any unusual swelling. Always listen to your gut; if something feels seriously wrong, it probably is. Remember, it's better to be cautious and seek help rather than wait and see if things improve.

When faced with an emergency, being able to clearly communicate what's going on can be life-saving. Practice explaining what happened simply and directly. If you're calling for help or speaking to an adult, mention who is affected, what the symptoms are, and where you are located. It can be nerve-wracking to think on your feet, but staying calm helps. Speaking slowly and clearly allows the person on the other end to understand your situation better. Also, if you're with friends or family, assign someone to stay with the affected person while others get help; teamwork makes a huge difference.

Preparation can significantly improve your response in urgent situations. It's a great idea to learn basic first aid skills and familiarize yourself with emergency numbers. Consider creating a small emergency kit with essentials like a flashlight, band-aids, and a whistle. These tiny steps make a huge difference when every second counts. Being prepared not only builds your confidence but also equips you to handle unexpected challenges with a cool head.

The Importance of Staying Informed

Technology in the Wild: Good or Bad?

Using technology during outdoor adventures can be both a blessing and a challenge. On one hand, gadgets like GPS units, smartphones, and safety apps can guide you through the wilderness, help you find your way back if you get lost, and keep you in touch with your friends or family. Imagine climbing a mountain and using an app that tracks your progress or shares your location with a buddy. That's pretty cool! However, relying too much on technology can lead to problems. If you focus too much on your screen, you might miss the beauty around you, like the rustling trees or the sound of a babbling brook. Plus, if your device runs out of battery or loses signal, you might feel more lost than ever.

Finding the right balance between technology and nature can make your outdoor adventures more enjoyable and safe. One strategy is to set specific times for using technology, like checking your phone for messages or using a compass app only at designated rest spots. This way, you can take advantage of the benefits of technology without losing touch with the natural world. When you set out for an adventure, consider leaving your phone in your backpack while exploring. Take a moment to identify trees, listen to animal calls, or sketch what you see. If you do need to use your device, think of it as a tool to enhance your experience rather than as the main attraction. This allows you to immerse yourself fully in the sights and sounds of nature while still having the safety net that technology provides.

Preparation is key when heading into the wilderness. Always let someone know where you're going and when you plan to return. Carry extra batteries or a portable charger for your devices so you're never completely cut off if something goes wrong. When hiking, consider using a map instead of only a GPS; this way, you develop skills that could come in handy if technology fails. Above all, trust your instincts. If a trail looks risky or if you feel uneasy about something, it's okay to turn back. Stay aware of your surroundings and enjoy the adventure! Learning to balance technology and nature not only keeps you safe but also enhances your experience, enriching your time outdoors.

Understanding Survival Apps and Tools

Survival apps are like having a trusty guide in your pocket, ready to lead you through the wild. Think about how easy it is to get lost in the woods or find yourself in a tricky situation. Several apps can help you navigate and build survival skills. For example, apps like Gaia GPS let you download maps and show your exact location, even without cell service. This feature is critical when you're exploring remote areas where getting lost can be dangerous. Additionally, apps such as Compass and Hiking GPS will help you learn how to use a compass, navigate using stars, and match what you see on the map with the landscape around you, improving your route-finding skills. There are also first aid apps like the American Red Cross First Aid app, which provides detailed instructions for treating common injuries and emergencies. Being prepared with first aid knowledge can make a difference in life-threatening scenarios.

When selecting survival apps, consider your specific needs and the type of adventures you plan to take. Look for apps that have positive reviews from other outdoor enthusiasts; they can give insights into how effective the app is in real-world situations. It's also smart to pick apps that work offline since not all locations have reliable cell service. Read through the app's features to see if it offers tools that you will find helpful. For instance, if you're interested in learning survival skills, seek out apps that provide tutorials or tips on building shelters or starting a fire. Finally, don't forget to practice with the apps before heading out. This helps build your confidence and ensures you know how to use each feature, preparing you to face challenges safely and effectively.

Being mentally prepared is just as important as your gear or the apps you choose. Survival situations can be overwhelming, but having the right tools can make all the difference. Always remember to have a plan and tell someone where you're going. Stay alert, think through your options, and no matter what happens, stay calm—you can handle it.

Preparing for the Unexpected: Stay Updated

Understanding the weather and knowing what's happening around you is crucial for anyone who loves adventure. It can determine whether your trip is fun or turns into a risky situation. For example, if you're hiking up a mountain and suddenly a storm rolls in, knowing about it beforehand can keep you safe. Keeping an eye on weather apps or local news helps you plan your activities wisely. Being updated on conditions like heavy rain or high winds can help you decide if it's better to stay in or adjust your plans. Also, familiarize yourself with local geography. Understanding the area can help you find safe spots if you're caught in an unexpected situation. Your knowledge about weather patterns and local conditions can make all the difference between a glorious adventure and a dangerous crisis.

Having a good communication plan is another key element of adventure safety. Before you set off, make sure everyone in your group knows how to get in touch with each other. Designate a meeting point in case anyone gets separated. Use reliable tools like walkie-talkies or a phone with a charged battery. Discuss what you'll do if you can't reach each other, such as waiting for a certain amount of time before heading back. It's smart to check in with someone who isn't going on the trip, letting them know your plans and expected return time. This person can help coordinate searches if things go sideways. Consider sharing real-time locations through phone apps, but always make sure your group agrees on safety and privacy boundaries. Good communication can be a lifesaver, making sure everyone stays on the same page even in unpredictable situations.

Remember, preparation isn't just about gear; it's also about information. Check the forecasts and local news regularly, even just before heading out. Knowing what to expect empowers you to make informed decisions. Stay curious about the outdoor world, and always keep learning how to navigate it safely.

Hiking Safety: Know Before You Go

A Family Hike Turns Hazardous

The Johnson family had planned their hiking trip for weeks. They packed their gear, checked the weather, and mapped out the trail. Excitement buzzed in the car as they drove to the trailhead. The sun was shining, and they were eager to explore the beautiful nature around them. As they started their hike, with their dog Max running happily ahead, everything seemed perfect. The trail was surrounded by tall trees, singing birds, and the sound of a nearby stream. However, as they climbed higher, the path became rocky and steep. Without warning, dark clouds loomed over the mountains, and a sudden storm changed everything. Rain poured down, making the trail slippery and dangerous. The family had to decide quickly how to stay safe while trying not to panic. Their adventure turned into a race against the weather, and they had to work together to navigate the tricky terrain. It wasn't just about reaching the top anymore; it was about getting back safely.

This experience taught the Johnsons important lessons about preparation and safety. They quickly realized that no matter how well they planned, the unexpected could happen. They had underestimated the weather, showing them the importance of checking forecasts closer to their trip and being ready for sudden changes. The family discussed the need for proper gear, like rain jackets, hiking poles, and sturdy shoes to handle the slippery rocks. They also learned to stick together and communicate clearly, which was crucial during the stressful moments. This not only helped them avoid getting lost but also boosted their confidence in managing scary situations. Even in challenging times, they realized the value of staying calm and focused. By adapting to the circumstances, they made it back to their car safely. Being prepared doesn't just mean packing supplies; it also includes being mentally ready for whatever nature throws your way. Understanding and planning for potential dangers can transform a fun outing into a life-saving experience.

When planning your next outdoor adventure, always consider what could go wrong and bring items to help you manage unexpected situations. Carry a small first aid kit, an emergency whistle, and extra food and water. And never forget that the best adventure is one that you get to share safely with your family and friends.

Planning Your Hike: Safety Checklist

Before you hit the trails, it's crucial to check off everything you might need for a safe and enjoyable hike. This checklist will help you prepare for any adventure, big or small. Start with the basics: make sure you have the right gear. A sturdy pair of hiking boots suited for the terrain will protect your feet and give you better grip. Remember to wear moisture-wicking clothing to keep you dry and comfortable. Packing a well-fitted backpack that's not too heavy will keep your energy levels up. It's important to stay hydrated, so fill up a water bottle or hydration pack, and don't forget some snacks to keep your energy up along the way. A map and compass, GPS device, or even a smartphone with downloaded maps can help you navigate. Always bring a first aid kit containing essentials like bandages, antiseptic wipes, and any personal medications. Make sure to pack a flashlight or headlamp for emergencies. Lastly, packing a multi-tool or knife can come in handy in various situations while you're out in nature.

Now let's talk about smart packing strategies to ensure safety while you explore the great outdoors. Organizing your backpack in a way that allows you quick access to items is smart. Keep your water and snacks in the top pocket or side compartments, making them easily reachable. Heavy items should be positioned closer to your back and centered for balance. As you hike, take regular breaks to hydrate and refuel, but also to assess your surroundings. Keep an eye on the weather, and don't hesitate to turn back if conditions worsen. Carrying a whistle can be useful if you need to signal for help. Mental preparedness is just as important as physical gear. Familiarize yourself with trail markers and keep an eye on your energy levels. If you're feeling tired, it's perfectly okay to adjust your plans. Sometimes, that means turning around or finding a shorter route. Always hike with a buddy if possible, as this not only provides companionship but also enhances safety in case of emergencies.

Understanding the possible dangers of the trails is key to prevention. Always be alert for changing terrain, wildlife, and weather changes. It's essential to know your limits; don't push yourself too hard. If you're encountering any difficulties, like a steep slope or slippery rocks, take your time and assess how to proceed safely. Mental resilience plays a big role in hiking. Keeping calm in challenging situations can help you think clearly and make better decisions. Use positive self-talk to boost your confidence when tackling tough moments. Take time to enjoy your surroundings; observe everything from the rustling leaves to the chirping birds. With the right preparation and a clear mindset, hiking can be a thrilling and safe adventure. Always remember: preparation is the best way to ensure you return home with great stories and memories.

Trail Etiquette: Staying Safe and Respectful

Respecting nature and other hikers is crucial for everyone's safety and enjoyment on the trails. When you step onto a path, you enter a shared space where both flora and fauna thrive alongside fellow adventurers. Each interaction you have can leave a positive impact or, if unthoughtful, lead to inconvenience or danger. Imagine hiking along a beautiful forest trail, only to see litter scattered about. That not only harms the environment but also affects the experience of those who come after you. By keeping the trail clean and taking only memories with you, you help preserve its beauty for future explorers. It's equally important to respect the wildlife you encounter. Meeting a deer or spotting a rare bird can be exciting, but approaching too closely can stress them out or cause dangerous situations for yourself and others.

There are some simple guidelines you can follow to ensure a positive experience on the trail. First, always stay on marked paths. This minimizes the impact on nature and helps prevent you from getting lost. When you come across other hikers, practice the trail etiquette of yielding the trail to those going uphill, which can be challenging. A smile and a friendly greeting can go a long way in making connections and creating a friendly atmosphere. Remember to share the space by keeping noise levels down; this allows everyone to enjoy the sounds of nature. Being aware of your surroundings also includes understanding potential dangers, like steep drops or sudden weather changes. Always check the forecast before you head out. Preparing for different trail conditions can mean the difference between a fun adventure and a challenging one. Carrying a simple first-aid kit and knowing how to use it is another way to protect yourself and others. Always keep mental resilience in mind. When facing obstacles or unexpected situations, remaining calm and focused will help you make the right decisions to ensure everyone's safety.

Lastly, the best way to ensure a safe and enjoyable hiking experience is preparation. Familiarize yourself with the trail maps and be ready for anything, from sudden changes in weather to encounters with wildlife. This will not only keep you safe but will also enhance your adventure, allowing you to fully appreciate the beauty of the great outdoors.

Survivor Stories: Lessons Learned

Tales of Heroism from Young Survivors

Young people often find themselves in situations that test their bravery, revealing stories of heroism that can inspire others. One such story features a twelve-year-old named Mia, who was hiking with her friends when they discovered a small boy lost in the woods. Despite the fear that gripped her, Mia remembered the survival skills she learned from her outdoor club. She rallied her friends, and they quickly set about searching for the boy's parents while keeping him calm. Their teamwork and clear communication made a daunting situation manageable. This kind of courage shows that even in frightening moments, young people can rise to the occasion, demonstrating that bravery isn't the absence of fear, but rather acting in the face of it.

The courage exhibited by young people like Mia can serve as a powerful motivation for others facing their own challenges. When we hear these stories, we understand that bravery comes in many forms and often involves simple but critical decisions, like remaining calm, thinking clearly, and looking out for one another. This kind of mental resilience is essential during emergencies. By sharing stories of heroism, we can encourage others to prepare for unexpected events. It helps them realize that they too can endure tough situations by adopting a mindset focused on problem-solving and empathy.

Preparation plays a vital role in surviving dangerous scenarios, and it's something anyone can do. Learning basic survival skills, such as how to find safe drinking water, build a shelter, or signal for help, makes a huge difference. Engaging in outdoor activities not only builds confidence but also sharpens decision-making and resilience. Even making a small habit of discussing safety plans with family or friends during outings can promote a culture of awareness. Remember, taking time to prepare today can help ensure that you're ready to face whatever challenges the future may hold.

Analyzing Key Decisions Made During Crises

Crises often come out of nowhere, turning ordinary days into moments that demand quick thinking and bold actions. During these times, certain decisions can mean the difference between survival and disaster. For example, imagine being caught in a sudden storm while hiking in the mountains. In that moment, the choice to seek shelter quickly could save your life. When faced with danger, individuals like explorers, first responders, or even everyday people rely on instinct and learned skills to navigate through critical situations. Each choice made in these crucial moments reveals the importance of preparedness, stealthy observation, and decisive action. Heroes are not always those who plan their decisions perfectly; they are often those who rise to meet an unexpected challenge with courage and calm. This courage during a crisis can redirect the path to safety and survival, emphasizing the vital role of rational thinking under pressure.

Creating a solid framework for decision-making in emergencies can make all the difference. First, it's essential to remain calm. Stress can cloud judgment, making it difficult to make sound choices. When you stay focused, you can assess your situation more clearly. Think about the options available and weigh their pros and cons quickly. For instance, if you're lost in the woods, determining whether to stay put for rescue or move toward a identifiable landmark involves critical thinking. Use the acronym STOP: Stop, Think, Observe, and Plan. This can serve as a helpful guide. Experts often stress the importance of preparation—learning skills like map reading, first aid, and weather patterns can fundamentally change your decision-making process. Furthermore, mental resilience plays a crucial role in these situations. It's about staying collected while trusting your knowledge and instincts. The ability to bounce back from setbacks during a crisis is what often leads to successful outcomes.

Always reinforce your learning with practical drills. Simulating emergency situations, whether it's through role-playing or outdoor activities, develops muscle memory and instinctive reactions that are invaluable when real crises arise. Preparing for the unexpected expands your capability to handle anything life throws at you. It's not just about facing danger; it's about cultivating a mindset geared toward survival and safety. Remember to look for sources of information, like survival guidebooks and local training programs, to build your experience and knowledge further. The more prepared you are, the better equipped you will feel when a challenging situation arises.

How Survival Stories Inspire Future Generations

Survival stories have a powerful way of capturing the imagination, especially for young people. When teens hear about real-life adventures where someone faced great danger and overcame it, they feel a spark of excitement. These tales often feature heroes who use their wits, skills, and courage to make it through tough situations. This connection to adventure inspires youth to dream big and think about the adventures they can embark on themselves. Whether it's hiking in the wilderness, camping under the stars, or simply exploring nature at a local park, survival stories show that adventure is all around us and that anyone can face the unknown.

Every story of survival teaches valuable lessons about preparation, quick thinking, and resilience. Young readers can see how each decision made during a critical moment can lead to safety or danger. They learn that adventure is not just about the thrill, but also about being responsible and making informed choices. These lessons resonate and encourage young adventurers to think about what they need to pack, how to stay aware of their surroundings, and what to do if things don't go as planned.

The excitement of adventure is complemented by the understanding that with the right preparation and mindset, they can tackle challenges head-on.

Sharing experiences from survival stories is essential for helping others learn and prepare. Storytelling can take many forms, from writing blogs and articles to creating videos or leading community workshops. By talking about what went wrong in an adventure and how it was handled, people can gain insights that might help them avoid similar mistakes. Whether it's sharing tips on how to navigate using a map or discussing the importance of having a first-aid kit, the act of sharing knowledge builds a community of prepared adventurers.

Peer-to-peer learning is particularly powerful for this age group. Young explorers can teach each other valuable skills, such as how to build a shelter, start a fire, or signal for help. Organizing group activities like camping trips or survival skill challenges encourages teamwork and built confidence. These shared experiences reinforce the message that while adventure can be exhilarating, it should always be approached with respect for nature and an understanding of potential dangers. By fostering a culture of safety and preparation, survival stories turn into educational tools that empower future generations to explore the great outdoors with confidence and respect.

Consider keeping a journal when you go on your own adventures. Write down what you learn, the challenges you face, and how you overcame them. This practice not only helps you reflect on your experiences but can also serve as a valuable resource to share with others who are eager to learn about survival skills and safe exploration.

The Journey Ahead: Lifelong Survival Skills

Continuing Your Adventure: Resources for Learning

Finding the right resources to learn about survival skills can feel like an adventure itself. Libraries and bookstores often have sections dedicated to outdoor skills, survival tactics, and bushcraft. Many of these books feature tips and techniques written by survival experts who have spent years honing their craft. You might discover classic titles by authors like Bear Grylls or modern guides that break down survival skills into easy-to-follow steps. Additionally, online platforms like Amazon or Goodreads can connect you with book reviews and recommendations tailored to your interests, helping you choose the best materials for your adventure.

In addition to books, there are numerous online courses available through sites like Udemy, Coursera, and even specialized survival websites. These courses often include video tutorials, quizzes, and interactive elements that make learning engaging. Local outdoor organizations often host workshops or courses, too, where you can get hands-on experience while meeting others who share your enthusiasm for the outdoors. Community forums, like those on Reddit or specific Facebook groups, are fantastic places to find like-minded individuals who can share their insights and experiences.

Learning about survival doesn't have to be all serious; it can be fun and exciting too! Many YouTube channels focus on survival skills and outdoor adventures, featuring experts and enthusiasts alike. These channels often demonstrate techniques in real-world settings, making the lessons feel alive and relevant. Watching these videos can spark your imagination and prepare you for your own adventures.

There are also exciting apps designed for outdoor enthusiasts. Some offer navigation tools and survival tips right at your fingertips, while others include games that teach you about wildlife, plants, and survival strategies in a playful manner. You might also enjoy podcasts that feature stories of survival situations, sharing both thrilling accounts and expert advice. These engaging stories not only provide valuable lessons but also highlight the importance of mental resilience and preparedness for any situation.

As you dive into these resources, remember that learning is an ongoing journey. Embrace the adventure of discovery and know that each new skill enhances your ability to navigate the great outdoors safely. One practical tip: always practice your skills in a controlled environment before you venture into the wild. This way, when a moment arises that tests those skills, you'll feel ready and confident.

Building a Community of Young Adventurers

Finding friends who are excited about outdoor adventures can be a rewarding journey. One of the best ways to start connecting with others who share your passion is to join local outdoor clubs or groups. Many communities have hiking, camping, or adventure clubs where young people gather. These places are great for meeting like-minded peers. You can also look for online forums or social media groups dedicated to outdoor activities. Here, you can share your experiences and get to know others who enjoy exploring nature.

Another effective way to connect with peers is through school or community events focused on outdoor activities. Many schools host weekend adventure programs or outdoor education days. Participating in these events allows you to meet other students who have similar interests. Don't hesitate to invite friends to join you in a new outdoor activity, like rock climbing or kayaking. Sometimes just suggesting a small weekend hike can surprise you with how many of your peers might want to join in.

When planning group activities, choosing the right adventure is important. Start by discussing interests with your friends. Do they prefer hiking, biking, camping, or perhaps water sports? Once you have a common interest, work together to plan the event. If you choose a hiking trip, research trails that suit everyone's skill levels. It's important to ensure that the chosen path is safe and suitable for your group. Always talk about what gear you'll need, such as proper footwear, water bottles, and snacks.

In addition to outdoor adventures, consider making it an event that involves the whole community. Organizing a clean-up day at a local park can be a fulfilling way to bond while giving back. You can also invite friends to a skills workshop, like learning to set up a tent or safely start a campfire. Learning together can strengthen your friendships and build confidence in new skills. Remember to discuss safety rules before heading out on any adventure. Understanding the risks and how to handle them is crucial, so always prioritize preparation and talk about everyone's concerns together.

As you plan outings, focus on creating an inclusive environment. Encourage everyone to take part and emphasize teamwork. Setting up a buddy system during your adventures can help keep everyone safe and ensure no one gets left behind. Building a community of young adventurers means looking out for each other, sharing knowledge, and creating memories that will last forever.

For a practical tip, always have a plan in place. Know the location, understand the potential risks, and create a checklist of what to take. This way, you can fully enjoy your adventure without worrying about forgetting something important. Always remember, preparation is the key to enjoying the great outdoors safely.

Embracing Outdoor Experiences Safely

Nature is a powerful teacher, revealing its wonders to those willing to explore. When you step outside, you're opening the door to a world full of adventures. However, this exploration can come with risks that need to be managed. Understanding the importance of safety while engaging with the great outdoors means you can enjoy these experiences without fear. It begins with simple actions, like dressing appropriately for the weather and always having the right gear. For instance, sturdy shoes are essential for hiking to prevent injuries, while a light jacket can save you from sudden changes in temperature.

Before setting out, it's crucial to communicate your plans. Share where you're going and when you expect to return. This not only ensures someone knows your whereabouts but builds responsibility for your own safety. Additionally, take the time to learn about your destination, whether it's a local park, forest trail, or mountain. Researching the area helps you understand any potential hazards so you can be better prepared. For example, if you're hiking in an area known for wildlife, knowing how to react if you encounter an animal can make a big difference in your safety and peace of mind.

Exploring the outdoors offers the chance to make amazing memories that last a lifetime. Imagine hiking up a mountain and reaching the summit; the view you see can be breathtaking. But what makes those memories even better is knowing you were responsible and safe while making them. Creating these positive experiences involves being aware of your surroundings, sticking to marked trails, and leaving no trace behind. When you take care of the environment, it shows respect for the place you're exploring and ensures that it remains beautiful for others.

Engaging in outdoor adventures also builds resilience. When you're out there facing challenges, whether it's navigating a tough trail or pitching a tent for the first time, each small success adds to your confidence.

Surrounding yourself with friends or family can enhance these experiences, as teamwork and shared excitement lay the foundation for unforgettable moments. Remember stories of those times in the wild can teach you about problem-solving and creativity, especially when plans change or obstacles arise. Encouraging each other to stay safe while trying new activities ensures everyone can enjoy the journey together.

As you prepare for outdoor adventures, remember that the best experiences come from a mix of excitement and mindfulness. Carry a first aid kit and know basic first aid techniques. This preparation isn't just smart; it's empowering. When adventure calls, being ready means you can focus on the fun while embracing the natural world around you.